# Dental Drill Art

## A Beginners Guide To High Speed Engraving & Carving

By Roger F. Wolford

Copyrighted 2016 – Roger F. Wolford

The author copyrights the photographs and patterns contained herein. The patterns contained may be scanned and used by the reader but not reproduced for resale.

Carving and engraving with the dental drills inherently includes risk of injury and product damage. This book and the author do not guarantee or warranty the contained projects and the dental drills are safe for everyone. Therefore, the author disclaims any liability for injuries, losses, or damages caused in anyway by the contents of this book and the tools discussed within. Planning and practicing thoroughly can greatly reduce most risk in every project. Please plan ahead and wear the proper personal protective equipment for you projects.

*I dedicate this book to my wife Angie and my boys (Ben and Seth). It cannot be easy listening to me ramble on about turbines, burs, handpieces and so on.*

*Thank you.*

# About The Author

The dental drill has chiseled a lasting impression onto my artwork and me.

I have always had a drive to create art and design but it was the dental drill that allowed me to engrave and carve my artwork on almost any surface I wanted.

I began using the dental drill in 1995. I purchased my original equipment from the back of a woodworking magazine and was hooked to dental drill art from the start. It opened up so many new opportunities for my artwork and me. Shortly after receiving the dental drill I opened a small home-based business engraving and carving for locals around my hometown. It was a very exciting time in my creative life. Every day I was learning new techniques and methods for engraving and carving different materials and items. Suddenly almost everything I looked at became a possible canvas for my dental drill art.

After over two decades of using the dental drill I still enjoy it as much as I did the first day the truck delivered the equipment to my doorstep. I have the fortunate pleasure of working with knife makers, furniture makers, gun collectors, antique collectors, business owners, and everyday people just wanting one of a kind items engraved or carved. My carvings have been featured in magazines and newspapers both locally and internationally. I love creating art with my dental drill and others seem to also enjoy it. What a great journey this has been!

**Website:** ROGERWOLFORDSTUDIO.COM

# Preface

Throughout my years of using the dental drills I have encountered many others also wanting to make art with the dental drill but do not know where to begin or find the subject too intimidating to start. I continue to get emails and messages from people wanting help and advice on the drills and getting their dental drill art hobbies started. It was this strong need that prompted me to put together this book.

Reflecting back on the beginning of my own dental drill art journey I wish I had some sort of a structured guide myself. If some of the information in this book would have been available in my early years it could have had saved me time, frustration, and some costly mistakes. All of which that I do not wish for you, the readers, to repeat.

 The information in this book has come from websites, blogs, social media post, Internet videos and other various sources on the web. I have also interviewed other dental drill artist, spoke with the many manufactures of the dental drills and drew from my own personal experiences. I then pieced all of this information together in hopes of giving the inspiring newcomer something they could use to guide them into the creative world of dental drill art.

My wish is that this book will aid in the start of new dental drill artist that will experience the great joy of creating with the drills as I do. The dental drills are very versatile tools and I'm sure there are many fantastic ways of using them that have yet to be discovered. I look forward to the new art and new ideas this next generation of artist will bring to the world of dental drill art and hopefully this book helped.

# Before we begin…………

In this book the dental drills are often called handpieces, high-speed drills, ultra high-speed drills and just drills. They are all referring to the same type of tools and the names are interchangeable.

I also interchange the words carving and engraving in his book. It is a fine line between the two when talking about the dental drills. Engraving is usually just work on the surface and carving is much deeper work. The dental drills can do both and the boundaries between the two often get blurred.

I have no affiliation, nor have I received any compensation, from any of the manufactures or companies mentioned within this book.

In the "Handpiece Review" section I write specific details about the individual dental drills. Otherwise, I'm using generalizations based on the majority of the handpieces and their designs to describe them elsewhere in the book.

On many subjects within the book I give my personal opinion. My opinions are based on my experiences with the equipment I have owned and the type of carvings I perform. Other dental drill artist may have a different opinions based on their own personal experiences and their type of artwork.

# Table of Contents

- Introduction..................................................Page 7
- The Dental Drills.........................................Page 9
- The Air Turbine..........................................Page 12
- Handpiece Reviews....................................Page 15
- Handpiece Tips...........................................Page 29
- The Burs.....................................................Page 30
- The Air Compressor...................................Page 34
- Shop Setup.................................................Page 36
- Personal Safety..........................................Page 37
- Image Transfer..........................................Page 39
- The Artwork..............................................Page 42
- Woodcarving..............................................Page 43
- Eggshell Carving........................................Page 45
- Bone, Antler, & Tagua...............................Page 49
- Gourd Carving...........................................Page 51
- Glass & Metal Engraving...........................Page 53
- Step-By-Step Projects................................Page 55
- Conclusion.................................................Page 84
- Resources..................................................Page 85

# Introduction

### What is "Dental Drill Art"?

Simply put it is art created primarily with a pneumatic dental drill. Dental drill manufacturers produce straight shaft dental drills for dental lab use. Those drills are also excellent for artist and craftsman. The straight shaft drills use the same little drill burs that your local dentist uses on your teeth. Instead of drilling away cavities, artist use them to drill away glass, metal, wood, bone, antler, and other surfaces to produce images, shapes and lettering.

Is this Dental Drill Art?

### Why use a dental drill for art?

The high speeds of the dental drills and the variety of burs allow artist to engrave and carve in great detail very efficiently on practically any surface. Surfaces such as hard woods, knife metals, antler, and glass can be engraved or carved almost as easy as writing with an ink pen. The high speeds produced by dental drills overcome obstacles like hard wood grains and tempered steel with ease. Electric drills rotate at lower speeds causing drag or pull while used on harder surfaces. This can cause difficulty when engraving or carving in detail. The dental drills traditionally are also much smaller, lighter, with less vibration than their electric counter parts.

Some artists use a combination of electric drills (low-speed) and pneumatic dental drills (high-speed). Electric drills can use larger burs that are preferred in removing large amounts of material to rough in shapes. The high-speed dental drill would then be used to add the finishing details that require more control and accuracy. I personally use both but my high-speed dental drill is in my hand about 80% of the time when I engrave or carve. If the dental drill can be used over my electric motor I will choose it every time. It gives me more control of my work and it is more comfortable to use.

## Who can be a dental drill artist?

If you enjoy being creative and making things I would say a straight shaft dental drill is a good tool for you.

Some dental drill artists just use it for a fun hobby. Some use it as an engraving and carving business to make art and personalized items. Others use the drills as an addition to their other hobbies. For examples I know knife makers, furniture makers, gunsmiths, jewelers and wood turners who use the dental drills to take their craft to the next level and set themselves apart from the rest.

I have always had a drive to make some sort of art. I always enjoyed drawing pictures and designs. When I came across the dental drill I saw it as a great way to get my art onto objects much more interesting and marketable than just paper or canvas.

Some traditional wood carvers make the switch to dental drill carving because it is easier on their bodies. Using the traditional carving knives and chisels can take toll on your muscles and joints. Using the dental drill takes little muscle effort making this a less strenuous hobby.

## Where can I be a dental drill artist?

The answer to this question is: about anywhere with an electric outlet.

To make a workspace to be a dental drill artist does not require a large area. You just need enough room for an average size table or desk. It is nice to have a large studio or dedicated shop but it is not a necessity. My workshops have been in spare rooms, basements, sheds, and garages. Some of these may have not been the best setups but it did not keep me from creating good carvings and engravings.

Some dental artist takes the show out on the road. If you can find a power outlet you can setup shop and carve and engrave about anywhere. You can personalize items at malls or department stores. Give demonstrations at art and craft shows. I have found that most people love to watch other people create and they are more likely to purchase your items if they get a glimpse at the process.

# The Dental Drills

The modern dental drill, or dental handpiece, is a high-speed drill that can rotate up to 400,000 revolutions per minute using an air turbine. These drills are usually about the size of a large marker and require compressed air to rotate the turbine. The high speeds of the air turbine are what produce the "ear-piercing shrill" that usually invoke fear in most dental patients. But for dental drill artist that same sound can invoke inspiration and creativity rather than cavity nightmares. From personal experience, I have seen that feared "ear-piercing shrill "gather groups of potential customers at art and craft shows. People know that sound and have to understand why it would be somewhere other than a dental office.

Traditional dental drills are designed with a 90-degree angle to help the dentist get to your teeth in your mouth. Straight shaft drills are designed for

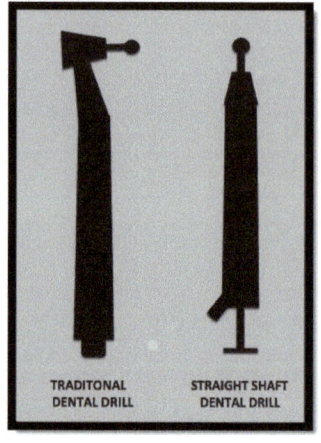

working outside the mouth in the dental labs.

There are many styles and companies of straight shaft dental drills on today's market. If you search "high speed dental drill" or "high speed engravers" you will find new and used straight shaft dental drills that range in price for $185-$600 US dollars each for the handpiece.

When considering buying an artist dental drill you have options and a few things to consider.

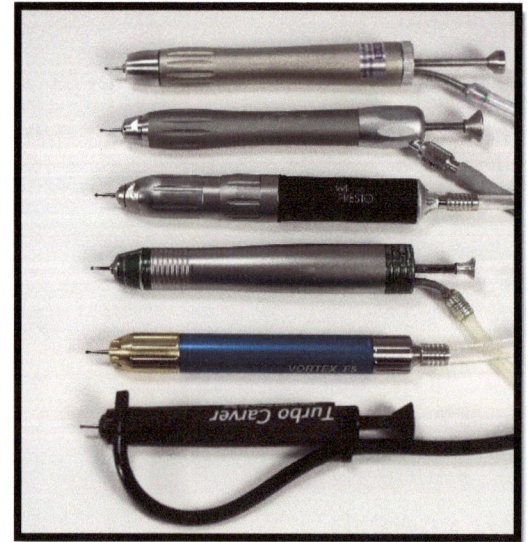

The first is what will your primary medium be? The dental drills are very versatile and will work on most any surface but some drills have a bit more power than others. The extra power may be needed for materials like wood, antler, or bone. Certain drills offer accessories and attachments they may give you an advantage on your medium of choice. For example, some have water mist attachments that aid in keeping eggshell and antler dust down and others has guide attachments that keep the drill perpendicular to your surface for a router type application that is useful for cutting straight lines and edges in wood signs and lettering.

Another consideration is noise level. If you carve in public you will want a quieter drill. While that "ear-piercing sound" can bring customers in, it can also drive them away if it is too annoying. Also please be kind to your family or roommates! If your shop is in earshot of others give them a break. My family was most appreciative when I switched to a quieter model of dental drill.

Also consider ergonomics. The dental drills are light, fast and efficient but you still may be carving for multiple hours at a time. Keeping yourself comfortable is important to your well-being and to the quality of your work. It is difficult to produce nice art with a cramped hand.

Last but not least, I suggest researching the company that sells the drill. Are they a reputable company? Do they offer support? Do they have aids to help with first time setup? Do they have good instructions to help you maintain your drill? Do they stock replacement turbines? These are the things that will make your life easier and keep your carving and/or engraving experience less stressful.

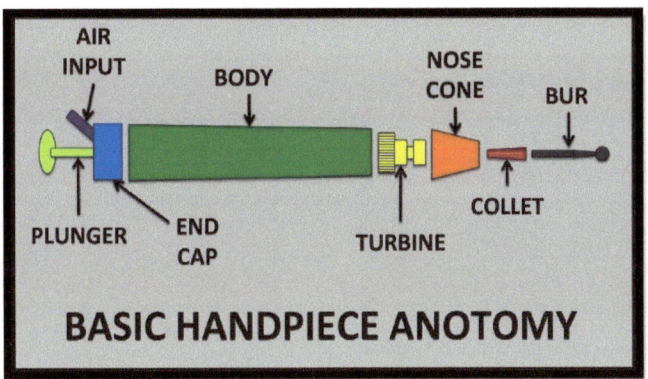

Many companies sell "systems or packages" that include most the items to get you started as a dental drill artist bundled into one large package. These usually also come with one large price. They can range from around $500 to $5000 US dollars. This is where you will need to weigh convenience verses cost. If you want to get going fast and don't want to deal with the hassle of shopping this may be worth it for you. If you are more patient and frugal you can breakdown the package and shop around. You may find you already own some of these items currently. For most of the dental drills the only necessary components to start carving and engraving is: an air compressor, the regulator and moisture trap, the dental drill handpiece, a few burs to cut with, and some air hoses to connect it all together. Everything beyond this is option you may or may not find useful depending on what type of work you will be doing.

If you are curious as to which handpiece I'm currently using please go to my website or social networking pages. I would be happy to answer any questions you may have regarding the dental drills and my experience I had with the models I have owned.

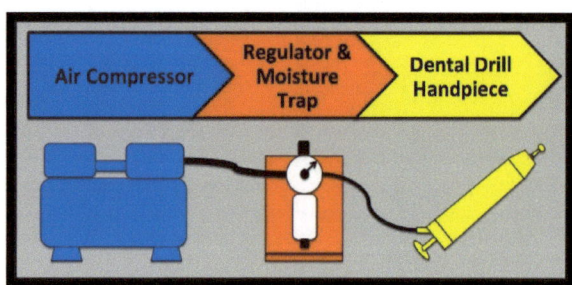

I have reviewed 6 popular handpieces in this book. Hopefully my experiences can help guide you to the best dental drill for you and your art.

In the reference section I have listed various websites where you can begin shopping for the high-speed headpieces and accessories. If you do your research well and weigh your options I'm sure you will find the drill that is right for you.

# The Air Turbine

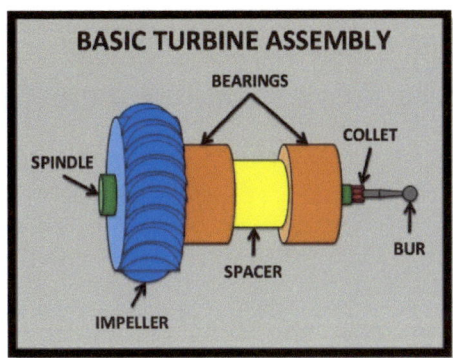

The air turbine is the engine of the dental drill. It is located in the nose cone of the drill and is what makes the bur rotate so you are able to cut at the high speeds. The drills range from 300,000 to 400,000 revolutions per minute (RPM's). Most electric motor hand pieces average about 30,000 RPM's. The dental drills are about 10 times faster than their electric counter parts.

You do not need to be a turbine engineer but it is a good idea to know a bit about how the air turbine works. You may need to do the preventive maintenance as per the manufactures recommendations. Personally I like to at least know what I'm looking at and what the functions of the parts are.

Generally the main components of an artist dental turbine are the spindle, (2) ball raced bearings, spacer, and an impeller. These components and their arrangement can vary by different models and manufactures.

Air flows in through the air input stem, then through body of the dental drill. The fan like blades of the impeller catch the compressed air as it flows over the turbine assembly producing the rotation of the bur that is seated in a collet within the spindle. The air usually exhaust out of the nose cone and out the end cap. Some models only exhaust out of nose.

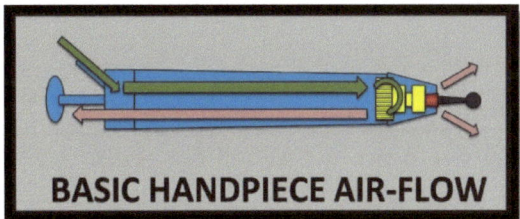

The speed of the bur rotation is controlled by the amount of air pressure entering the handpiece. By adjusting the air regulator you can change the speed of your turbine and the burs. All dental drills have a recommended not to exceed air pressure. This is to protect premature failure of the turbine components. Please follow the recommended guidelines for your model.

Slowing down the RPM's is useful while performing fine detail work and sanding but about 80% of the time I run my drills at their recommended maximum air pressure.

**Sealed vs. Oiled Bearings**

When you search the Internet for the straight shaft dental drills you will find there are companies selling sealed bearing turbines and the oiled (wet) bearing turbines in their drills.

The oiled bearings require oil added into the airline ever so often to properly keep the bearings lubed. With some oiled drills this is done manually using a bottle dropper and others use an in-line oil reservoir to automatically add a drop or two a minute as you work directly into the airline. The pressurized air moves the oil through the airlines and into the bearings of the turbine.

The sealed bearing dental drills have bearings that contain oil already sealed into the bearing assembly. Therefore require no oil to ever be added.

The oiled bearing turbines claim to last longer than the sealed bearing systems but the oil can be messy. The sealed bearing turbines are cleaner and generally require less maintenance than the oiled version. There is much debate on which of these systems are truly the best for engraving and carving.

I used an oil drip system for almost 15 years before I switched to an oil less system. Now that I have made the switch, I prefer not to return to the oil drip. For me, it is just more convenient not dealing with the oil.

## Turbine Failure

Turbines can fail due to many reasons. Abuse and poor maintenance seem to be the main causes. I have had a few of my own turbines fail. I think it was just a case of old age and maybe a bit of abuse on my part. One day my bur just stop spinning in mid-cut and that was the end of it. I found a few companies online that sold replacement parts but I was not brave enough to attempt rebuilding this on my own. I shipped it to a professional and he rebuilt it for about half of the cost of a new turbine. Most generally it is the bearings that go bad and someone who is experienced with the proper tools can replace them fairly easy (see resources section).

I always keep a spare turbine on hand. If my turbine happens to go bad I do not want to miss important customer deadlines. To me this is well worth the price. I could not imagine telling a bride that I will not be able to engrave her custom wedding glasses on time because my turbine is in the shop.

# Handpiece Reviews

I have listed reviews on 5 handpieces commonly used by dental drill artist and 1 newly released handpiece that I was curious about (Vortex F5). All of the handpieces reviewed are owned and purchased by myself. I have no affiliation with any of the manufacturers of these handpieces and have not received any compensation from them. I'm simply a consumer giving my personal experiences and observations using these tools.

There is a lot of different opinions and talk online as to which handpiece is the best and I really wanted to find out for myself. If you do the math you will notice I have spent some cash on my collection. My hope is that my experiences can help inform you in picking the best handpiece on the first purchase and save you trouble, time, and money.

While there may be some drawbacks with some of these handpieces they all can create great art within their range of capabilities. Remember, these are all high speed drills made for very detailed precise work.

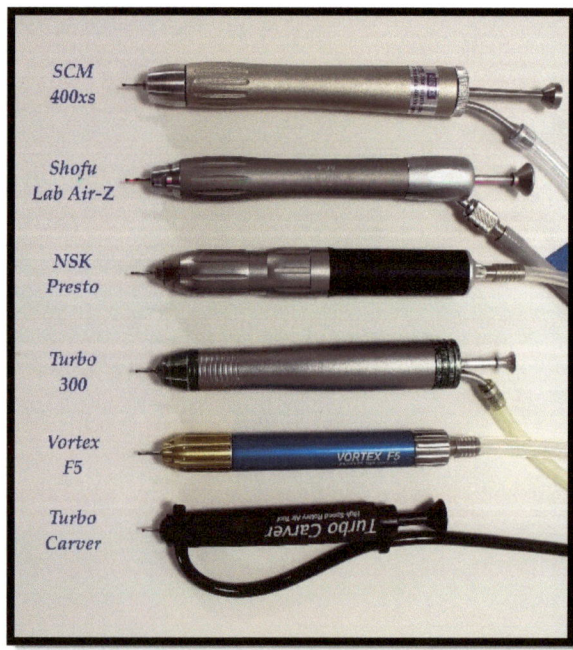
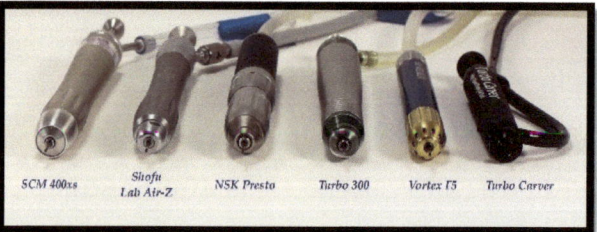
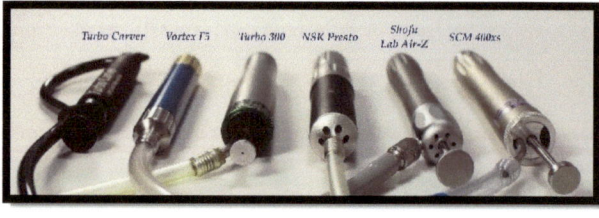

# SCM 400XS

**Weight:** 3.00 oz.
**Lengths:** 6.00 inches
**Decibels:** 73.9db @ 12"
**Max RPMs:** 400,000
**Max PSI:** 37
**Avg Handpiece Price:** $550 USD

Pros:

- Low Decibels
- Low Maintenance
- Warranty
- Sealed Bearings
- Power
- Router Base

Cons:

- Non Rebuildable Turbine
- Nose Cone Size
- Cleaner Drops

**Company and Warranty:** The 400XS handpiece is sold and built exclusively by a company named SCM Engraving. SCM has been selling and servicing handpieces since 1988. They provide product support and training materials for first time setup and equipment operation. SCM provides a 1-year limited warranty on the turbine and a limited lifetime warranty on the handpiece.

**Power:** The 400XS has good power. The SCM 400XS performs well in glass, eggshell, gourd, wood, and bone. I rate it at a high level of power.

**Turbine:** The 400XS uses a sealed bearing turbine but it is not rebuildable. SCM does sell a replacement turbine cartridge for around $200 USD. I have not tested my 400XS long enough to personally vouch for the durability but I have interviewed other owners that have 5 years or more on their original turbine.

**Maintenance:** SCM recommends adding one drop of a cleaner into the airline every hour of use with a bottle dropper. The cleaner is to remove small particles that might enter the turbine assembly thru the airlines. It evaporates and does not affect your working surface or make a mess. This task is not a big deal but I find it hard to remember to do this every hour while I'm working.

**Author's Notes:**

SCM makes an attachable router base for the 400XS. I find this very handy for carving consistent depths like sign lettering and making straight lines using a ruler or guide.

The 400XS has the largest diameter nose cone of all handpieces I have reviewed. It is about 7/16" in diameter. It is noticeable when working with the tool and can block your view. It occasionally can cause interference when it is necessary to carve at 45-degree angle or less.

It is the third most expensive handpiece in my reviews. Only $50 USD less than the highest priced Turbo 300. I have noticed that SCM will sometimes have sale prices on their handpieces. If you watch their website you may be able to get this at lower than the sticker price.

The 400XS is the largest handpiece in my review. Depending on your size of hand this could be a positive or a negative.

It has low decibels and would work well for a travel handpiece for public demonstrations and on-site engraving or carving.

Out of all 6 of the handpieces reviewed the SCM 400XS is one of the most powerful.

# Shofu Lab Air-Z

**Weight:** 3.00 oz.
**Lengths:** 5.35 inches
**Decibels:** 73.2db @ 12"
**Max RPMs:** 360,000
**Max PSI:** 35
**Avg Handpiece Price:** $490 USD

Pros:

- Comfort
- Low Decibels
- No Maintenance
- Sealed Bearings

Cons:

- Warranty
- Non Rebuildable Turbine

**Company & Warranty:** The dental supply company Shofu produces The Shofu Lab Air-Z handpiece. The Shofu handpiece is sold by websites like Arizona Gourds and Graphic Transfer and they both provide customer support and first time setup instructions. Shofu provides a 90-day limited factory warranty.

**Power:** The Shofu performs well in glass, eggshell, metal and gourd. It lags a bit in wood. I consider the power of the Shofu a medium level.

**Turbine:** Shofu uses a sealed bearing turbine. It is not rebuildable but can be replaced with a new cartridge for around $200 USD. I have owned my Shofu for about 1 year and cannot personally vouch for the durability but I have interviewed other owners that have 5 years or more on their original turbine.

**Maintenance:** The Shofu handpiece requires no maintenance.

**Author's Notes:**

This handpiece has one of the smallest nose cone of all the handpieces reviewed. It measures about ¼" in diameter. The small nose is covenant for engraving or carving at 45-degree angles or less. When performing very small detail work the Shofu works very well.

The Shofu has a slim comfortable design, and is quiet. It has fairly low decibels and would work well for a travel handpiece for public demonstrations and on-site engraving or carving.

# NSK Presto

**Weight:** 2.50 oz.
**Length:** 5.25 inches
**Decibels:** 72.7db @ 12"
**Max RPMs:** 320,000
**Max PSI:** 35
**Avg Handpiece Price:** $390 USD

Pros:

- Low Decibels
- Sealed Bearings
- Rebuildable Turbine
- Twist Action Bur Release

Cons:

- Air Exhaust
- Warranty
- Turbine Durability

**Company & Warranty:** The dental supply company NSK produces the NSK Presto. Engraving and carving websites like Profitable Hobbies, Treeline USA, and Utah Handpiece Repairs sell this handpiece. The NSK Presto comes with a 90-day limited factory warranty.

**Power:** The NSK Presto performs well in glass, eggshell, gourd, wood, and bone. I rate it at a medium-high power tool.

**Turbine:** The NSK Presto uses a sealed bearing turbine. The turbine is replaceable and rebuildable. A new turbine assembly cost around $160 USD and the rebuild is about half of that price. I personally have rebuilt my turbine twice in three years of use but I push my turbines pretty hard while relief carving wood. If you are just surface engraving glass and metal then the turbines should last longer.

**Maintenance:** NSK recommends cleaning the turbine and collet after about 40 hours of use. This requires disassembling the nose cone and removing the collet. There are a few very small parts that have to be removed and I am always nervous of loosing or damaging them in the process of the maintenance.

**Author's Notes:**

The NSK uses a twist action to eject the bur. I personally like this design over the traditional plunger style. The bur literally jumps right out of the handpiece when released.

The NSK is one of the quietest handpieces. It would work well for a travel handpiece for public demonstrations and on-site engraving or carving.

The handpiece design places the air input centered in the end cap and prevents the airline from interfering with hand placement. This allows for more freedom of movement and comfort while trying to carve or engrave. This tool is popular with those doing freehand engraving due to this freedom of movement.

The NSK exhaust most of the air out of the rear of the tool and little out of the nose. That means the NSK blows very little dust away as you carve and engrave. This causes me to have to stop very frequently to clean off my carvings or engravings to see my work.

# Turbo 300

**Weight:** 2.35 oz.
**Length:** 5.00 inches
**Decibels:** 90.5db @ 12"
**Max RPMs:** 350,000
**Max PSI:** 45
**Avg Handpiece Price:** $ 600 USD

Pros:

- Power
- Durable
- Rebuildable Turbine
- Router Base

Cons:

- High Decibels
- Oily
- Maintenance

**Summary:**

**Company & Warranty:** A company named Profitable Hobbies exclusively sells the Turbo 300. Before they were known as Profitable Hobbies they went by Paragrave and Paragraphics. They have been selling and servicing handpieces since 1983. They provide customer support and training for setup and equipment operation. Profitable Hobbies provide a 1-year limited warranty on the handpiece and turbine.

**Power:** The Turbo 300 has good power. It performs well in glass, metal, eggshell, gourd, and wood. It can even tackle the relief carving in the hard woods like gunstocks. I rate it at a high level of power.

**Turbine:** The Turbo 300 uses open (wet) bearings for its turbine. This requires an in-line oil drip to keep the bearings properly lubed. An oil reservoir drips about 1-2 drops of green oil every minute of use. The turbine can be replaced for about $335 USD and rebuilt for around $100 USD.

The handpiece pictured is an older model of the Turbo 300. According to Profitable Hobbies, it has the same turbine as the current model sold today. I purchased this handpiece in 1995 and it still runs well. I have pushed this tool very hard and have only had to rebuild the turbine once in over 15 years of use. It has been a reliable tool.

**Maintenance:** This style of a turbine requires a bit more maintenance then the sealed bearing systems. This involves removing the turbine and collet and manually cleaning about every 40 hours of use. The disassembly is not difficult but is an oily process.

**Author's Notes:**

Profitable Hobbies sell an attachable router base for the Turbo 300. I find this very handy for carving consistent depths like sign lettering and making straight lines using a ruler or guide.

While the oil drip is part of the reason this is a reliable tool, it also can be a nuisance. The oil can get onto your working surface and your hands during use.

This tool is not as covenant as the sealed bearing dental drills for a travel. If the oil reservoir gets tipped over during transport you may have an oily mess to deal with.

The decibel levels are the highest of all tools reviewed. I personally do not like to use this tool without ear protection.

The Turbo 300 is one of the most powerful handpieces reviewed.

This is the most expensive tool in my handpiece reviews.

# Vortex F5

**Weight:** 2.00 oz.
**Lengths:** 4.50 inches
**Decibels:** 86.6db @ 12"
**Max RPMs:** 400,000
**Max PSI:** 38
**Avg Handpiece Price:** $595 USD

Pros:
- Twist Action Bur Release
- Air Input Placement
- Nose Air Exhaust
- Warranty
- Sealed Bearings
- No Maintenance
- Rebuildable Turbine

Cons:
- Unestablished
- High Decibels

**Company & Warranty:** The Vortex F5 is exclusively sold on the website Sculpting Studio owned by the company Unbridled. Released into production in November 2016, it is the newest high-speed handpiece on the market today. The Sculpting Studio builds and services the Vortex F5. The Sculpting Studio provides a 1-year limited warranty on the turbine and a lifetime warranty on the handpiece.

**Power:** The Vortex F5 performs well in glass, eggshell, metal, wood, gourd, and bone. I rate the power of the Vortex F5 at a medium to medium-high level.

**Turbine:** The Vortex F5 uses a sealed bearing turbine. It is replaceable and rebuildable.

**Maintenance:** The Vortex F5 handpiece requires no maintenance.

**Author's Notes:**

The Vortex F5 design is very slim yet still feels sturdy. It is only ½" in diameter and 4 ½" long with a nose cone diameter of ¼". I have a medium size hand and find it comfortable. But someone with larger hands may have issues with its small slim design. However, those of you with smaller hands would most likely find this a good fit.

It uses a simple but covenant 1/4 twist action end cap to load and release the burs. This is the only handpiece you do not need to press the bur into the collet. You just twist the end cap to release the bur, insert a new one and twist back to lock the bur in.

It exhausts all of the air out of the nose pushing the dust away from the carving area very well. I find this feature very handy while woodcarving.

The Vortex F5 tested as the second loudest handpiece. Like the Turbo 300 I do not like to run it without hearing protection.

Much like the NSK Presto, it has placed the air input centered in the end cap allowing it not to interfere with hand placement. Also much like the NSK, I feel this tool would be good for freehand glass engraving due to the freedom of movement.

I know color does not make a handpiece perform better but it does raise a few eyebrows and I find it worth mentioning. My family gave the Vortex F5 some big "oohs and aahs" when I first showed it to them.

The Vortex F5 handpiece is too new on the market for the durability and dependability of this tool to be established at this point in time.

The Vortex F5 is the second most expensive handpiece reviewed. It is only $5 USD cheaper than the most expensive Turbo 300. I have noticed that the Sculpting Studio has reduced price sales often and you may be able to get this a bit cheaper than the sticker price if you watch their website.

The Vortex F5 I used in this review is a prototype model that I received from the Sculpting Studio ahead of their production run. They picked customers to send the first 10 handpieces to for early feedback. I was one of those 10. The Sculpting Studio has assured my handpiece is the same as the current production model sold on their website today.

# Turbo Carver

**Weight:** .55 oz.
**Length:** 4.00 inches
**Decibels:** 86.8db @ 12"
**Max RPMs:** 400,000
**Max PSI:** 40
**Avg Handpiece Price:** $185 USD

Pros:

- Price
- No Maintenance
- Sealed Bearings

Cons:

- Non Rebuildable Turbine
- Low Power
- High Decibels
- Plastic Construction
- Air Hose Placement

**Company & Warranty:** The Company Turbo Carver produces the Turbo Carver handpiece and provides customer support and first time setup instructions. The handpiece can be purchased at Turbo Carvers website and also other websites like Arizona Gourds, Chipping Away, and Woodcarvers Supply. Turbo Carver provides a 6-month limited warranty on the handpiece and turbine.

**Power:** The Turbo Carver has the least amount of power of the handpieces reviewed. It performs fair in glass, metal, and eggshell but struggles in wood, gourd, and bone. I rate it at a low power level.

**Turbine:** Turbo Carver uses a sealed bearing turbine. Turbo Carver can rebuild the turbine for around $85. They do not offer a replacement turbine cartridge but replace the entire handpiece instead. I have not owned my handpiece long enough to vouch for its durability but my interviews with other dental drill artist lead me to believe it is less than the other handpieces in this review.

**Maintenance:** The Turbo Carver handpiece requires no maintenance.

**Author's Notes:**

Turbo Carver offers a water mist option that allows a fine mist of water to be sprayed on your bur and working surface as you engrave to keep the dust down. I do not own the water mist system but I can see how this could be beneficial when carving eggshell and glass.

Turbo Carver runs its airflow to the turbine external of the handpiece body. This places the airline in a position that interferes with hand placement. I personally find this distracting and the airline interferes with my work when using burs that require a 45-degree or less angle.

Turbo Carver's rubberized grip is a nice touch that I wish the other handpieces also had.

The Turbo Carver is mostly made from plastic. It does not feel as sturdy as the other handpieces reviewed.

The Turbo Carver is the least expensive handpiece reviewed.

# Author's Ratings

I have constructed a matrix to rate the 6 dental drill handpieces from my reviews. It is based on my experiences and observations while using them in my shop. I have scored them in eight categories I consider most important to my satisfaction as a consumer. To add weight to the score, I assigned each of these eight categories a factor based on their level of importance to me.

### Weighted Handpiece Matrix

| Handpiece | Power | | Durability | | Turbine | | Warranty | | Decibles | | Comfort | | Support | | Maintenance | | Total Score |
|---|---|---|---|---|---|---|---|---|---|---|---|---|---|---|---|---|---|
| Importance Factor | 5 | | 5 | | 5 | | 3 | | 3 | | 5 | | 4 | | 3 | | |
| SCM 400XS | 5 | 25 | 4 | 20 | 3 | 15 | 5 | 15 | 5 | 15 | 2 | 10 | 5 | 20 | 3 | 9 | 129 |
| Shofu Air Lab-Z | 3 | 15 | 4 | 20 | 3 | 15 | 1 | 3 | 4 | 12 | 4 | 20 | 5 | 20 | 5 | 15 | 120 |
| NSK Presto | 4 | 20 | 2 | 10 | 2 | 10 | 1 | 3 | 5 | 15 | 5 | 25 | 4 | 16 | 2 | 6 | 105 |
| Turbo 300 | 5 | 25 | 5 | 25 | 3 | 15 | 3 | 9 | 1 | 3 | 3 | 15 | 5 | 20 | 1 | 3 | 115 |
| Vortex F5 | 4 | 20 | 3 | 15 | 3 | 15 | 5 | 15 | 2 | 6 | 5 | 25 | 3 | 12 | 5 | 15 | 123 |
| Turbo Carver | 1 | 5 | 2 | 10 | 2 | 10 | 2 | 6 | 1 | 3 | 1 | 5 | 5 | 20 | 5 | 15 | 74 |

**Weighted Category Score (bold) = Score X Importance Factor**

**Total Score= Sum of (8) Weighted Category Scores**

**Highest Score Possible = 160    Lowest Score Possible = 32**

| Importance Factor | | Score Criteria | |
|---|---|---|---|
| 5 | Very High Importance | 5 | Very Best |
| 4 | High Importance | 4 | Good |
| 3 | Important | 3 | Fair |
| 2 | Low Importance | 2 | Low |
| 1 | Very Low Importance | 1 | Lowest |

I scored the power of the dental drills based on how they perform in glass, metal, eggshell, gourd, wood and bone. Relief carving in wood and bone generally requires more power than working with glass, metal, and gourds. You may visit my Youtube channel to see the videos of how I tested the drills for the power ratings. If you are not interested in carving wood and/or bone then your importance factor and/or score may be different than mine. If so, this will change the total scores of the handpieces for you.

Due to the Vortex F5 being so new to the market it was scored fair in the durability, turbine, and support catergories. Customer experiences and time may change these scores for the Vortex F5 in the future. The other 5 handpieces have been on the market for at least 10 years and have been well tested in these catergories by consumers.

# Handpiece Tips

Here are a few things you can do to help keep your dental drills in top condition.

- Never exceed the manufacturers recommended PSI. Cranking up that PSI beyond recommendation can damage or destroy the bearings in your turbine.

- Don't force it; let the burs do the work. If the turbine is bogging down or slowing down just back off or use a new bur. This is hard on the bearings.

- Keep the moisture out of your bearings. The air compressors will produce moisture and it can damage your turbine bearings. Always use a moisture filter, check it often, and keep it drained.

- Never use a bent or damaged bur. This can trash the bearings in your turbine. If a bur sounds or feels odd get it out of your handpiece. It is not worth the risk of damaging the turbine.

- Clean the dust off your nose cone prior to changing the bur. This can reduce the amount of debris that may get into your collet. I just use a small paintbrush and give the nosecone a quick dusting before ejecting the bur.

- Prevent your handpiece from getting dropped. This can damage the turbine. Especially if it lands on the nose. Do whatever you can to place and secure your airlines where they won't get tangled or tripped over. Use a handpiece cradle to keep it from getting knocked off your bench.

## The Burs

Burs, burrs, bits, cutters? I'm not sure what the actual names of these are. I have even seen the manufactures call them by two different names in the same catalog. For the sake of simplicity I will call them burs (with only one "R").

At first glance the choices of all the types of burs and which ones to use can be overwhelming. Don't freak out. It is not as complicated as it looks.

All of the high-speed drills use a bur with a 1/16 inch diameter shank. The 1/16" shanked burs must be rated for 300,000- 400,000 RPM's to safely work with the dental drills. Please only use the proper burs for your drill (see resource section).

The burs are held in the handpiece by the grip of the collet only. Therefore they are referred to as "friction grip" burs or "FG" for short.

Keep these details in mind while shopping. If you buy your burs from a website that specializes in high-speed engraving you will not need to worry much. They should only stock 300,000- 400,000 RPM, friction grip, 1/16" shank burs or at least have them in their own category. But if you shop at a website that sells general dental supplies you may need to filter down to find only these specific burs.

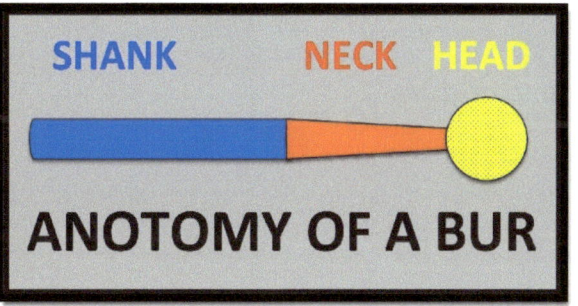

To load most burs into the drill you generally start the end of the shank by hand then push the head against something solid until it is fully seated into the collet. This should not require much pressure. I usually use a piece of hard wood to do this. Just be sure you do not use anything that will damage the bur head.

Burs that have a sharp tip and that are very fine will require a gentler touch. I will grip the neck of the bur with a pair of needle nose pliers to push the bur into the collet. This will help to keep from breaking the sharp tip of these types of burs during loading.

The various makers of the dental drills have different methods of ejecting the bur. Most have a plunger. This is just a rod that runs through the body of the handpiece and pushes the bur out of the collet. Another method is a twist action that releases the bur from the collet. You just twist a section of the handpiece and the collet releases the bur.

The three main materials that the bur heads are made from are carbide, 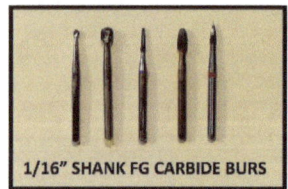 diamond, and stone. All of these come in many shapes and sizes. The most important thing to remember is that the bur material must be harder than the worked surface. For example, carbide burs work great in wood, glass, and tempered steel but you will not be successful using carbide on titanium steel. The titanium is harder than the carbide and will not cut it. Diamond, on the other hand, is harder than the titanium and will engrave the surface.

Carbide burs have blades cut into the head. The blades are cut in various angles and patterns to cut and scoop away the material. Carbide is about 3X's harder than steel. They are great for cutting and shaping wood, eggshells, gourds, bone, and antler. They are even used to engrave glass.

The valley between the blades can fill up with material causing poor performance. You can clean out the built up material by using a small wire brush. I just hold the shank between my fingers and clean the head with the wire brush.

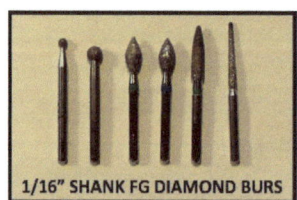

Diamond burs have diamond grit bonded to the head. The diamond grit works in a sanding action for engraving glass or smoothing and shaping in wood, eggshells and gourds. Much like sand

paper, they are available in different grits from extra fine to super coarse. Most companies identify the grit level with a colored band on the neck of the bur. If a diamond bur does not have a band it is most likely medium grit.

Also much like sandpaper the diamond grit can get loaded up with material. When this occurs the diamond will begin to burn the surface rather than sand it. You can open the grit up by lightly touching it to a dressing stone while the bur is rotating in the handpiece. Use this sparingly because over dressing can prematurely wear out the diamonds.

Stone burs are generally used at lower speeds and can be used on most any surface. They are good for polishing and smoothing.

Other than the hardness rule, there is nothing stopping you from trying any bur on any surface you want. Find what works for you. I keep scrap pieces of material laying around just to practice on. I try different burs and speeds until I get the desired effect I want.

All burs come in various shapes and sizes. Much like their name, there also is no standard as to what these are called. Some companies have a numbering system and some do not.

The closest burs to having a standard would be the "rounds". These are the ball shape burs. They are available in diamond and carbide. They are described by a numbering system, #2 round, #6 round, etc. The size of ball bur head progressively gets larger as the number ascends.

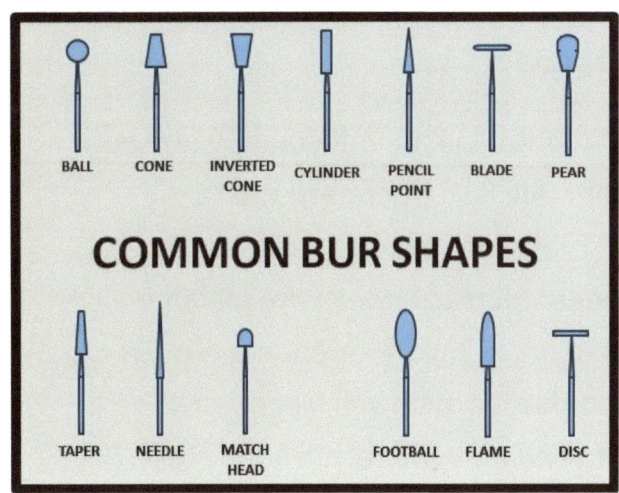

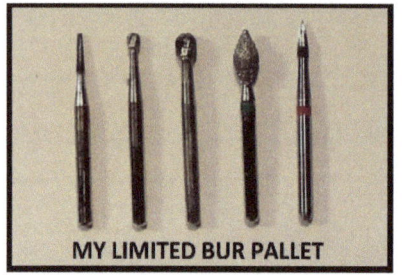

MY LIMITED BUR PALLET

If I had to limit my bur pallet to only five burs they would be:

- #699 Carbide Taper
- #4 Carbide Round
- #8 Carbide Round
- Large Diamond Football
- #7901 Pencil Point

I primarily work in wood but these five burs would also work well for about anything thrown at me. I have many other burs in my pallet but these are the ones that send me into panic if I run out. This is what works for me and may not be the perfect pallet for you but I bet they would be a good start.

I cannot exactly tell you how long a bur will last. There are too many variables to predict. Pressure, speeds, feeds, surface, these are all large factors in the life span of a bur. Of course, carbide will last much longer if used in wood rather than steel. Pay attention to how well it cuts and how much force you have to use. Once you tune into what a used up bur feels like you will know when to toss them.

There are many places that sell the high-speed burs. Just search "dental burs" on the Internet and explore. Generally the cheapest place to buy them is from dental supply websites.

Carving supply websites also sell burs. They are usually more expensive than the dental supply folks but they have done much of the sorting for you to ensure you get the proper burs for your drill.

Due to the lack of standardization, I find shopping for burs frustrating. With new suppliers you have to decipher their methods of labeling and sizing. Personally I prefer to find a supplier I'm pleased with and stick with them. This way I do not need to learn a new labeling system each time I purchase burs.

## The Air Compressor

All of the high-speed artist dental drills require an air compressor. They are pneumatic tools due to the required pressurized air to spin the turbines.

The dental drills have a few requirements that will determine the minimum style of compressor you will need. As you research this subject you will notice something called CFM's and PSI. CFM stands for cubic feet per minute. It is a method of measuring the movement of air volume over a period of time. PSI stands for pounds per square inch. PSI is a measurement of the air pressure.

The high-speed drills have requirements such as 1.0 CFM's at 45 PSI. That means you will need at least 1 cubic feet of air per minute while you run at 45 pounds of air pressure per square inch to properly run your handpiece. While this is good to know it may not take you far. It is tough to research air compressors by CFM output. Some list it and some do not. I will make this a bit simpler for you. Most ¾ horsepower air compressors have what it takes to run the dental drills. If you want to be 100% sure buy a 1 horsepower motor, or above, and you will be fine.

Now that we have established the minimum horsepower for the compressor, it is time to think about what to buy. Will you travel with it and use it at shows? Will it only be used in your shop? Will the noise level be an issue? What is your budget? These are questions that should drive what you purchase.

If you already own an air compressor and it is at least ¾ HP go ahead and start with that. See if it will fit your needs. Maybe borrow a friend's compressor for a while to get the feel for what will work in your shop.

The noise level of air compressors is measured in decibels (dB). A normal conversation at 3 feet is about 60-65dB. The average chain saw at normal use is 120db. If you are going to be at shows or your shop is in earshot of others you will want to consider the noise level of your compressor. If the compressor manufactures are not bragging about their decibel levels then you can bet it is going to be loud.

If you are a smart phone user, you can download "decibel meter" apps onto your phone. Not sure how accurate they are but they do seem reasonably correct. I have a ¾ HP compressor that measures about 62dB. I also have 4 HP compressors that run at 95dB. This is a 33dB difference but it is very huge to the unprotected ear. The 62dB is barely noticeable but the 95dB rattles your teeth. Don't take this subject lightly because you may have to live with it a long time.

Another option to cut down on noise is to buy a compressor with a storage tank. These are big and heavy. Not something I would consider for travel but are great for shop use. The motor of the compressor pumps air into a holding tank. Once the tank is full of compressed air, the motor shuts off and all is quiet. As you draw down the stored air from the tank the motor kicks back on to replenish. The larger the tank, the more horse power of the motor, the less it will run and the less noise you and those around you will endure.

Example of an air compressor with a tank

Example of a tank less air compressor

The tank less compressors run continuously. You turn them on with a switch or foot pedal, as you need the air. Because of their size and weight they are perfect for travel or tight spaces. They can be packed into a medium sized box or suitcase. Be sure to check for decibel levels while shopping for these. Just because they are small does not mean they are quiet.

# Shop Setup

We have talked about the drills, the burs, and the air compressors. Now it's time to put it all together and make the system run.

I will share with you a basic shop setup. This setup has served me well for many years. It is not the only way to setup shop but it is simple and effective.

I use a ¾ HP continuous (tank less) air compressor. It is maxed out at 100 PSI. The compressors power cord is plugged into a foot pedal switch and the foot pedal is plugged into a wall electrical outlet. So when I step onto the foot pedal it completes the electrical circuit and kicks on the air compressor power. When I lift my foot from the pedal it breaks the circuit and turns the air compressor off. I like the hands free operation of this setup. The foot pedals are available at about any hardware store.

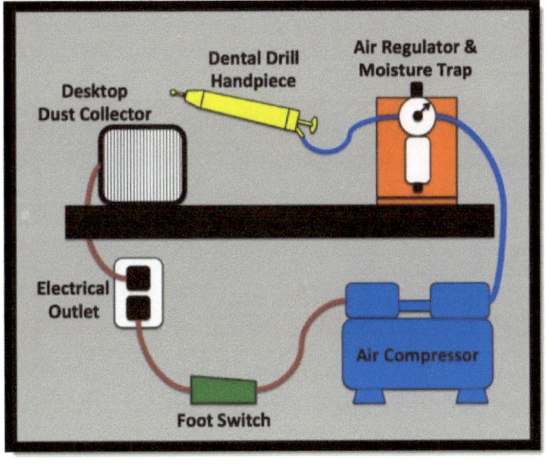

While the compressor is running it moves air to my regulator and moisture trap through an air hose. The regulator reduces the PSI to the required level needed for my handpiece. The air circulates through the moister filter trapping any water before the air leaves the unit.

The regulated and filtered air moves on to the handpiece thru a piece of flexible surgical tube rotating the turbine and bur allowing me to carve or engrave.

The moisture trap will need drained from time to time. If it gets too full then the water will get into your handpiece. This is bad for your turbine bearings. Be sure to check the moisture bulb often and drain as needed. In Illinois during the humid summer months I have to drain mine about every 30-45 minutes of use.

I keep a desktop dust collector on my workbench to help control dust and smoke as I work in addition to my personal protective equipment.

# Personal Safety

This is an important subject. To keep you safe and healthy for many years to come you need to take certain personal safety measures while you use the dental drills and other shop tools.

All of the dental drill manufactures will have their own safety recommendations for their tool. Please read them carefully and follow them as best as you can. I will share with you what I do in my shop.

As I have mentioned, the drills produce decibel levels averaging 75 dB or more. This is an OSHA acceptable level for 8-hour exposure but I would encourage you to protect your ears anyway. Let's play it safe and use some sort of earplug to block the sound during extended use. I know engravers who do not use ear protection but I prefer not to go without it.

When in my shop, I use a Bluetooth ear bud set. This blocks the sound and lets me listen to my music or podcasts while I work. Also, if I'm paired up to my phone I do not have to miss any important phone calls.

Eye protection, of some sort, is also important. The drill does produce particles that can get into your eyes. I usually wear a lighted optivisor

while I carve. It magnifies my work allowing me to see the details better but also gives some eye protection from flying particles. If I'm rough carving and do not need the magnification, I will use safety glasses or goggles.

The airborne dust. This is probably the largest issue with being a dental drill artist. No matter what material you work with there will be dust and keeping it out of your lungs, and anyone else's, is important. I wear either a dust mask or a respirator while I work.

**Listen to your snot!**

This sounds a bit nasty but it will tell if you are doing a good job of protecting yourself from the dust. It is snots job to keep the dust from entering our lungs. If you blow your nose after engraving or carving and find your snot full of dust then you are doing a poor job of protecting yourself and it is time to step up your game.

I use either a dust mask or a respirator depending on my project. The dust mask is good most of the time but eggshell carving and antler carving produce a dust that my snot tells me is too fine for just a dust mask. This is when I step up to the respirator.

I also run a desktop dust collector on my workbench and use an air filtration system in my shop.

When the weather allows I will open the doors and windows to keep the air flowing.

# Image Transfer

Image transfer is just like it sounds. You capture an image from one source and transfer it to your worked surface with the dental drill. This is why you will hear certain high speed engraving companies claim "if you can trace a line you can engrave" or "no artistic talent needed."

Not all dental drill artists use an image transfer method. There are some that have enough confidence to freehand their art directly onto the final piece. Personally I prefer to use a transfer method on all major projects. It allows me to ensure I have the proper proportions, alignment, and spelling before my bur even touches the worked surface. I carve or engrave many items that most likely could be done freehand but I prefer the extra layer of insurance that an image transfer provides. So far, there have been very few, if any, projects that I have totally botched.

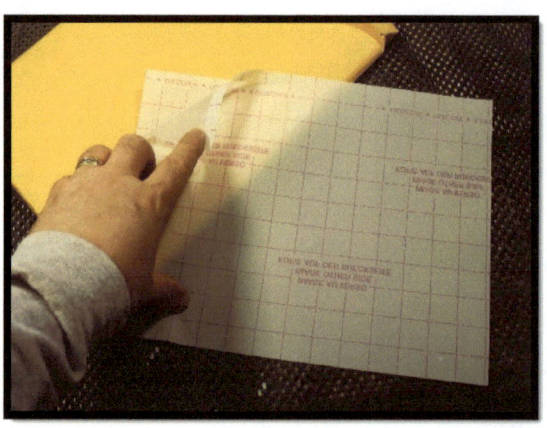

**Stencil Film**

The most common method of image transfer in the high-speed engraving world is the stencil film. Stencil film is a self-adhesive Mylar film. The film is basically a large piece of invisible office tape on a carrier sheet. It comes in standard 8.5"X11" sheets or large rolls. This film works great in copier machines and laser printers. Just scan your image and print it on the Mylar. Then peel off the backing sheet and stick the stencil film to your worked surface. The adhesive is repositionable allowing you to pick it up and move it multiple times to get the image aligned properly. Once you have it where you want it just trace the image with your dental drill and bur of choice. The drill will cut through the film and onto the surface underneath. Then peel off the film to see your engraved image.

The stencil film is a great way to transfer an image but I do not have a copy machine or a laser printer at home. Like most others, I own a home PC with an ink jet printer. I have tried to run the stencil film through my ink jet printer but the ink smears and will not dry. Prior to owning a home PC I used stencil film a lot. I made multiple trips to the library or the local copier store a week. Once I bought a PC that all seemed ridiculous with a perfectly good printer right at home. So I began to experiment and research ways to transfer an image with my PC and ink jet printer.

**Repositionable Spray Adhesive**

My favorite method to transfer an image is the "repositionable spray adhesive" method. The primary component of this method is an aerosol repositionable spay adhesive made by various manufactures including Krylon and 3M. It is available in most local craft stores or on-line. It usually cost from $8-$12 per can. One container will last me a long time. Be sure you get the "Repositionable" spray.

I print my image from my computer on normal 8.5"X11" printer paper or draw it in pencil freehand. I then cut the image out and lightly spray the back of the image with the adhesive.

These products turn my ordinary printed image into a repositionable sticker. I just stick it down and carve, or engrave, through the printer paper into my worked surface. Then peel away the sticker to reveal my work. Sometimes the adhesive can leave some gummy residue on the surface but it is easily removed with a bit of rubbing alcohol and a clean rag. It's cheap, effective, and simple.

Later on, in the step-by-step projects there are more examples of how to use the image transfer methods.

## Sticker Paper/Labels

My second most used method is almost identical to the stencil film method but is ink jet friendly. There are a variety of full-page sticker papers and labels available for the ink jet printers on today's market. Some are transparent similar to the Mylar used in stencil film. Those of you accustom to using the stencil film but want a more flexible method; this would be an easy transition.

I prefer using sticker paper when I have an image that I know I will be carving, or engraving, multiple times. I will fill a page, or pages, with the image and print it on the sticker paper. When I need it I just cut out the image, stick it down and transfer the image with my dental drill. Then file the rest away for the next time.

Ink jet sticker paper is available at some office supply stores but I find the best variety on-line. I have had good luck with "Avery #8665 Clear Full Sheet Labels" and "Avery #3383 White Sticker Project Paper".

# The Artwork

The Dental drill artist has a good way to capture and move artwork using the image transfer methods but be careful what artwork you snatch.

All I have to do is search what I want, when I want, on the Internet and there the image is on my screen. This is great but not everything on the web is just ours for the taking. Some images and patterns are copyrighted and using them in our works for profit can get us into trouble, even sued.

You can be inspired by other people's artwork and use that to create an original piece of your own, that's fine as long as it really is an original.

Or you can use royalty-free artwork made entirely by another Artist with the intent for someone else to use.

The Wikipedia definition of Royalty-free or RF is; *refers to the right to use copyright material or intellectual property without the need to pay royalties or license fees for each use or per volume sold, or some time period of use or sales.*

There are websites that sell royalty-free artwork and photographs either by the image or for a monthly subscription. Many of them have fantastic images that would work well for engraving and carving. You can also buy royalty-free images in printed books. Some of them are even designed specifically for engraving and carving (see the reference section).

Sometimes all you need to do is ask. There have been a few times I have came across a copyrighted photographs that I just had to have for a carving. I contacted the photographer and asked their permission to use the images. The majority of the time they are honored and will granted me permission. Out of respect for their original work I credited the photographer whenever I showed my carving.

I'm not a lawyer or expert on the copyright laws but I am aware of them and keep them in mind. If you decide to sell your dental drill art I urge you to educate yourself.

## Woodcarving

The dental drill allows wood carvers to work with hardwoods that traditional carvers usually shy away from. The high-speeds of the dental drill can tackle the hardwoods like walnut, maple, and hickory. In fact, the harder woods are where they perform the best.

Also because of the precision of the dental drills you can carve directly into a finished piece of wood. Only the area where you carve will be affected and then you just seal the carved area when finished. This allows us dental drill artist to carve on gunstocks, furniture, cabinets, jewelry boxes, and much more with little effort and in great detail.

Gunstocks are a popular medium for many dental artists. 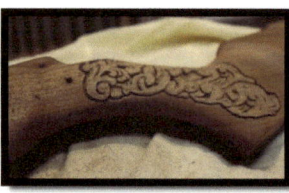 The hardwoods used in gunstocks are perfect for the dental drill. Also the dental drill artist can carve right over the top of the factory stamped checkering on the gunstocks with much more interesting designs. Wildlife scenes, farm scenes, clusters of leaves, old western scenes, scroll work, Native American designs, and so much more.

I work a lot with wood using my dental drill. I enjoy the amount of depth and detail I can pull out of the wood with the drill. I use the carbide burs for roughing in the images and the diamond burs for sanding and shaping the wood. I like experimenting with the burs to get various textures and designs in the wood to add contrast to my carvings.

 The finishing of the woodcarving is also a creative process. You can use artist oil paint, inlay materials, wood bleach, and wood stains to add various effects and depth to your carvings.

Wood has so many opportunities for the dental drill artist. I encourage all of you to give it try.

# Woodcarving Gallery

Log nameplate carved with a wolf and lettering.

Pheasant scene carved in a gunstock. Finished with oil paints.

Wood keepsake box carved with hummingbird and vines. Carvings inlaid with turquois liquid inlay.

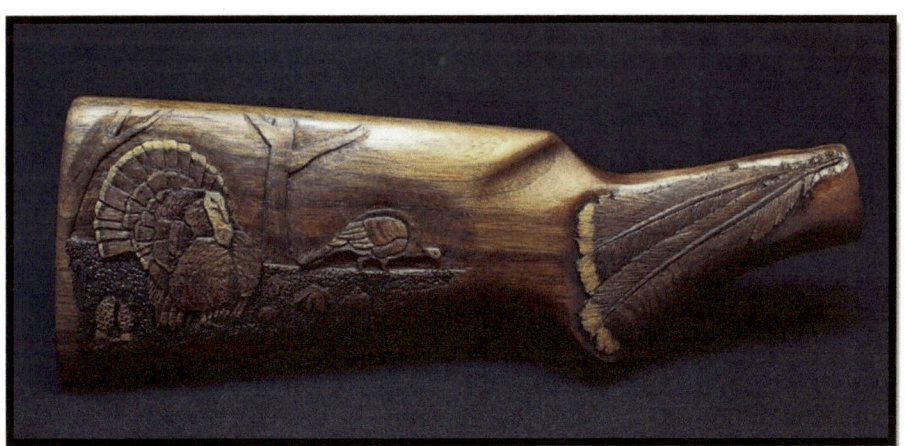

Turkey scene carved on a gunstock with carved turkey feather grips.

# Eggshell Carving

Yes eggshells. Real eggs laid by real birds carved by a dental drill.

Decorating eggs has been around for centuries in various cultures. They have been gifted and displayed for good luck, prosperity, and fertility. Many modern dental drill artists have carried on the fragile tradition taking it to new levels. The dental drill can cut amazingly intricate designs and images in eggshells leaving most people flabbergasted by the results.

Most eggshells can be carved but some are more suitable than others. Due to the thickness, the eggs of geese, duck, turkey, emu, rhea, and ostrich are my preferred shells for carving. Common store bought chicken eggs are generally too thin for a complex carving. The eggs of the larger varieties of birds are thicker and better to work with.

Even using the thicker eggs does not guarantee you wont break a few. This is disappointing, especially when you

have hours of time and energy in an eggshell carving. It is an eggshell after all, be gentle and handle them carefully and you can minimize the risk. This is what makes a finished eggshell carving so special. People find it hard to believe that anyone can do this without destroying the eggshell in the process.

I purchase my eggshells already cleaned and sterilized from farmers

on websites like Etsy and Ebay. The farmer drills a hole in the bottom of the eggshell and removes the yolk and sterilizes the shell for shipment.

Goose, duck, and turkey eggs are slightly larger in size than a chicken egg but have thicker shells. The emu, rhea, and ostrich shells are much greater in size and are the thickest. They can even be relief carved. I have experienced ostrich eggs that have been close to 1/8" thick.

The emu eggshell is very unique. It naturally has layers of color. The outside layer is a dark emerald green that gets progressively lighter the deeper you go, with the final

undermost layer being bright white. With proper planning the dental drill artist can take advantage of these colorful layers to carve beautiful eggshells.

When working with eggshells there are a few burs that I use often. The #699 carbide is great for cutting out pieces of the eggshell. I hold it perpendicular to the eggshell as I cut. For sculpting and shaping the eggshells I primary use the football shaped diamonds. I sometimes use the stone burs at a low PSI to polish the carved area. As always there are no set rules but

these are the burs I usually use for eggs.

You can use the image transfer methods with eggshell carving but because of the curved surface it can be difficult. If you use the image transfer you will need to cut it into smaller pieces. I prefer drawing with pencil rather then using stencils when working with eggs.

If the finished carving has cut outs I submerge the eggshell in bleach overnight. This whitens the shell but also dissolves the inner membrane that often is stuck to the inside of the shells. When finished I rinse the eggshell with warm water and let air-dry.

I always seal my eggshell carvings. I usually use a clear enamel spray. This protects the shell and keeps it from getting yellow over time.

There are various ways to display the finished eggshells. They can be hung with a hanger but most are displayed on a stand. There are special egg display stands for purchase on the Internet. Some even rotate and light up for a more dramatic effect.

Most eggshell carvings are protected behind glass display cases or under a glass dome. If I take an eggshell carving to an art or craft fair it will be protected under glass. Otherwise, someone might just walk up and grab it without asking. ☹

## What's that smell?

Eggshell carving does have its downsides. The shell is made from calcium carbonate and smells similar to burnt hair when carved. Not something most people enjoy. I usually wear a respirator while working with eggs.

Just like any other carving, eggshell carving produces dust but this dust is very fine. It can be dangerous so don't mess around.

As I said I buy eggshells that have been cleaned and sterilized but if you are not certain they were actually sterilized be sure to sterilize them yourself prior to carving. Eggshells can carry bacteria that can cause infection. You do not want to be breathing this stuff, so when in doubt, sterilize.

To sterilize an eggshell soak it in diluted bleach for a few hours. Then rinse with water and let air dry before carving.

If you can smell the fumes while carving then you are breathing in the dust. Adjust your respirator, open a window, and check the dust collector. Don't let that dust into your lungs.

If carving on eggshells bothers you no matter what you try, just stop and find something else to carve. Some people are allergic to the dust and cannot tolerate it. Listen to your body and respond quickly!

When I first began using my dental drill I hated working with eggs. Now that I have a good dust collection system and a proper respirator I find working with eggs just as satisfying and fun as working with any other material.

# Eggshell Carving Gallery

Goose egg

Emu egg

Emu egg

Ostrich egg carved with 3 barn owls and trees

# Bone, Antler, & Tagua

The dental drill can carve bone and antler very well. These materials are very similar to the teeth for which the drills and burs were originally designed.

I have used my dental drill to carve stag antler knife handles, bone and antler jewelry, scrimshaw, and more.

Bone and antler hold detail well and they can be carved and stained much like wood.

Another method available for the dental drill artist is scrimshaw. Scrimshaw is an ancient method of making images and designs in antler or bone using shallow scratches and filling the scratches with ink. Traditionally this is done using any sharp object and manually scratching the surface. The dental drill artist can be more efficient than the traditional scrimshaw artist by using pencil point burs or needle style burs and light touch to make the scratches. Thus making the job of scrimshaw easier on your arms and wrist.

*Deer scrimshawed on polished antler*

Much like eggshell carving, bone and antler carving produce a fine and smelly dust. Just like the eggs, I use a respirator and a dust collector while I work with these materials. Please refer back to the personal safety and egg carving sections for more details on this subject. Remember to listen to your snot!

Tagua nuts, or vegetable ivory, come from a tree in South America. They are a sustainable substitute for animal ivory. I have never carved on animal ivory so I cannot compare the two. However, I have carved many Tagua nuts and really enjoy working with them. It carves well but is less smelly than bone or antler.

# Bone, Antler, Tagua Gallery

Moose antler shed carved using an electric motor drill and a dental drill. Carving is painted with artist oil paints.

Tagua nut carved and inlaid with turquois liquid inlay.

Eagle feather carving made from sterilized cow bone.

## Gourd Carving

Some dental drill artists are "out of their gourds" for carving gourds! Okay, that's a bit cheesy but very true.

Carving and decorating gourds has been around for a long time. Many ancient cultures used hard-shell gourds for all kinds of things to make their lives more enjoyable. Eating utensils, containers, vessels, and musical instruments just to name a few. They love these dried woody fruits so much they began decorating them.

Today gourd art is an industry of its own. There are societies and festivals dedicated to this art form. They even make specialized tools and paints engineered specifically to perform on the hard-shell gourds. Just search "gourd art" on the Internet and be amazed at the cool things artist are creating with these unique fruits.

The hard-shell gourd (*Lagenaria siceraria*) grows in many shapes and sizes. When green the skins resembles the color and pattern of a watermelon. Once they are picked and dried the walls of the gourd turn into a substance that very much resembles and acts like a soft wood. This is one of the many reasons that dental drill artists are attracted to this carving medium. Our dental drills and dental burs perform well in the gourds and everything we know from carving wood also applies to gourds and vice versa.

I will not go into detail on how to prepare a gourd for carving. There are many books, blogs, websites, and videos on this subject already. If gourd carving interests you do the research and you will find the information you need. I have listed a few of these in the resources section.

I enjoy carving gourds. I find it very easy to turn a gourd into a piece of art. Nature has done most of the work for me and all I need to do is just add a bit of carving and color. I hope you and your dental drill give the hard-shelled gourd a try.

# Gourd Carving Gallery

Kettle gourd carved with spring turkey scene. Carving is painted with artist oil paints. Decorated with turkey feathers.

Kettle gourd carved with horse and rider scene. Carving is painted with artist oil paints.

Kettle gourd lamp carved with fall trees.

# Glass & Metal Engraving

In the 90's, when I first became a dental drill artist I did a lot of glass and metal engraving. Primarily, people wanted names and dates engraved on wedding glasses, beer mugs, knife blades, Zippo lighters and etc. Over time this has changed. Today people can order these types of items off of the Internet for a reasonable cost and fast shipping. I do not try to compete with the laser engraver folks. Instead I focus on what my dental drill can do that they cannot.

The dental drill can artistically engrave glass and metal where the computerized machines come out flat (pun intended). The dental drill artist can engrave letters and images in great detail on uneven and hard to reach surfaces. This is where the dental drill artist can shine in the glass and metal engraving world.

Another advantage for the dental drill artist is the capability to engrave one-off items fast and on the spot. We can be setup and engraving items in about an hour or less at craft shows, wine festivals, department stores and more.

A well-trained dental drill artist can personalize an item like a wine bottle or knife blade faster then it takes a laser engraver to just layout the job.

Diamond, carbide, and stone burs all work on glass and metal. The dental drill burs produce dents and scratches to engrave designs and lettering in the top surface.

To enhance some glass engravings I use a product called "Rub N Buff" made by the AMACO Company. This is a waxy metallic paste that comes in a variety of colors available at most art and craft stores and online. I rub a small bit of "Rub N Buff" over my engraved letters and/or images and then wipe away the excess. The "Rub N Buff" color remains in the engraved area adding color to my engravings. I use the antique gold or silver leaf colors the most.

# Glass & Metal Engraving Gallery

Champaign glass engraved with a feather

Engraved knife blade

Engraved Rifle

Personal message engraved on a bottle of wine. The engraving has been enhanced with gold leaf "Rub N Buff".

# Step-By-Step Projects

In this section I have included some step-by-step projects designed as an introduction to dental drill art. They are designed for various materials and subjects to help you explore the world of high-speed engraving and carving.

Even though these are entry-level projects they will take some practice. This is why I used easily accessible and cheaper materials for these projects. If you mess up throw it aside and start over. The important thing is to keep progressing and pushing forward. I have filled many garbage cans with my practice pieces. I have thrown my arms up and yelled "I suck!" BUT I never stopped. I have burned up diamond burs, I have snapped the heads off carbide burs, and I had to cover up my mistakes. This is all part of the learning curve a new dental drill artist goes through. It is how we establish the boundaries of our tools and push our talent to the next level.

**Okay...Let's make some dust!**

# 1. Lettering In Wood- "You Can Do This!"

Here is a basic wood carving method that most anyone can carve with some practice and, of course, a dental drill. Many times I have had my hand carved lettering mistaken for laser cut. While I take this as a compliment, I'm quick to tell them "it was hand carved."

This is a low relief wood carving of lettering with a simple image silhouette. This method will work on most any natural wood product that has been finished and sealed. I have used this method on gunstocks, furniture, small signage, cabinets, and nameplates. Take this process and practice your own name or phrase.

In this example I will be carving a nameplate made from a finished piece of poplar. It was sanded and sealed with semi-gloss polyurethane prior. This project took me about 15-20 minutes to complete. I choose the phrase "thumb up- you can do this!" because, well, YOU CAN!

**Supply List**

- Sealed Wood
- Repositionable Spray Adhesive
- Printed Text and Image
- Ruler
- High Speed Dental Drill System
- #699 Carbide Taper Bur
- #6 Carbide Ball Bur
- Plastic Scrapper
- Denture or tooth brush
- Burnt Umber Artist Oil Paint
- Semi-Gloss Polyurethane
- Medium Stiff Artist Paint Brush
- Small Detail Artist Paint Brush
- Clean Rags

**Step 1: Create the stencil.**

Layout your text and image in your preferred software and print it out on a normal sheet of paper. I used Microsoft PowerPoint for this example. Next spray the back of the image with repositionable spray adhesive and let dry about a minute. You now have a stencil sticker. See the "Image Transfer" section for more details.

**Step 2: Apply the stencil sticker.**

Stick the stencil onto the carving surface. Measure and reposition the stencil until it is centered and straight. Step back and look at it from a distance and be sure it is positioned correctly. Don't be afraid to reposition it multiple times to get it right. If needed, re-size the layout and start again.

**Step 3: Carve the outline.**

Use the #699 bur and outline around each letter and the image with the dental drill. Hold the drill perpendicular to the carving surface and plunge the bur about 1/8" deep. Do not force the bur.

Just let the drill do the work and guide it around the letters. Pull the drill towards yourself for better control.

**Tip:** While outlining the letters, it is best to carve the inside bowl of the letter "o" and "a" before carving around the exterior. This will prevent the pattern from moving before the entire letter can be outlined.

*Dental Drill Art*

**Step 4: Remove the stencil.**

Once all of the letters and the image have been outlined gently peel of the stencil by hand.

**Step 5: Remove any remaining stencil.**

Scrape off any remaining stencil with a brush or a piece of plastic. I'm using an expired credit card in the photo. Be sure to be gentle and not to harm or damage the worked piece.

**Step 6: Carve out the letters and image.**

Using the dental drill and a #6 carbide ball bur carve out the inside of the letters and the silhoutte. For the best cutting results hold the drill at about a 45 degree angle. Plunge the #6 ball into the

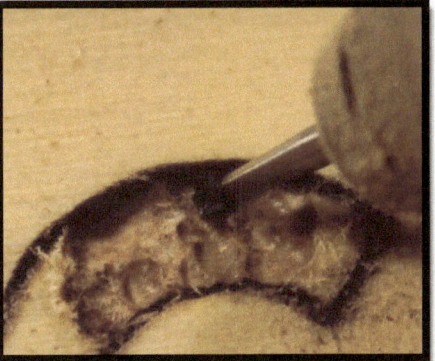

lettering and clean out the areas between the outlines, dropping the letters below the working surface. Drop carve the letters about 1/8" deep using a stippling* motion to acquire a rough texture in the bottom of the carving.

*Stippling is a dotted like pattern achieved by using a up and down motion while carving with a round bur.*

**Step 7: Clean the carving.**

Remove the sawdust and the little fuzzies from the carving. Use a medium to hard bristle brush and scrub off the carvings. Use enough pressure to remove the carving fuzzies but not enough to damage the worked piece. I'm using a denture brush in the photo.

**Step 8: Prepare for finishing.**

Inspect your work for areas that may need more carving. Look at the carving from every angle checking for missed spots and areas that are too shallow. Once you are satisfied with the carving, blow the carving off with compressed air. Be sure it is free of dust and contamination.

### Step 9: Mix the color.

Squeeze a small amount of burnt umber artist oil paint onto a piece of disposable cardboard or thick paper. Using a stick or pallet knife mix in the polyurethane until it becomes about the consistency of ketchup. I prefer using Windsor & Newton artist oil paints.

### Step 10: Scrub in the color.

Using a medium sized stiff bristled artist paintbrush apply the color mixture in the carved areas. Scrub it down in the lettering and silhouette covering all carved surfaces. Don't worry about getting the color on the non-carved areas. It is sealed and will wipe clean.

### Step 11: Wipe away the excess color.

Using a clean rag wipe away the excess color from the non-carved areas. An old t-shirt works great for this application.

The color will be absorbed into unsealed carved areas while the sealed surface wipes clean.

**Step 12: Touch up the color.**

Using a small detail artist paintbrush go over the carving adding more color in the carving as necessary.

**Step 13: Let the color dry.**

Allow the color mixture to dry at least 24 hours or until dry to the touch. Once it is dry you are finished.

# Finished Photos:

# You REALLY Can Do This!

👆 You Can Do This !

👆 You Can Do This !

👆 You Can Do This !

👆 You Can Do This !

# 2. Layers In Wood- Oak Leaves

For this project we will use layers to give our carving a more realistic look. Carving objects that are overlapping will make our work more interesting, and adding color can give it more depth.

I'm using oak leaves for this project. Many artists have long used oak leaves in carvings and engravings. I have used them in my own carvings on gunstocks, cabinets, walking sticks, and many other projects.

I'm using the oak leaves in this project to trim out lettering. The lettering is carved using the same method as I used in the "You Can Do This" project. I will only be focusing on the oak leaf carving for this example. Also like the last project, I'm using a finished piece of poplar wood for the carving.

**Supply List**

- Sealed Wood
- Repositionable Spray Adhesive
- Printed Text and Image
- Ruler
- High Speed Dental Drill System
- #699 Carbide Taper Bur
- #4 Carbide Round Bur
- Large Coarse Grit Diamond Football Bur
- Large Medium Grit Diamond Football Bur
- #7901 Pencil Point Finishing Bur
- Handheld Pin Vise
- Lead Pencil
- Tooth or Denture Brush
- Pre-Stain Wood Conditioner
- Satin Polyurethane Sealer
- Burnt Umber Artist Oil Paint
- Artist Paint Brushes
- Clean Rags

**Step 1: Create the stencil.**

Layout your text and image in your preferred software and print it out on a normal sheet of paper. I used Microsoft PowerPoint for this example. Next spray the back of the image with repositionable spray adhesive and let dry about a minute. You now have a stencil sticker. See the "Image Transfer" section for more details.

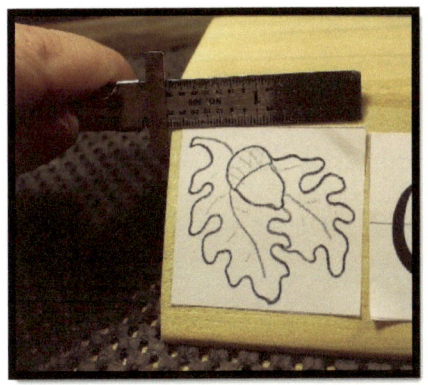

**Step 2: Apply the stencil sticker.**

Stick the stencil onto the carving surface. Measure and reposition the stencil until it is centered and straight. Step back and look at it from a distance to be sure it is positioned correctly. Don't be afraid to reposition it multiple times to get it right. If needed, re-size the layout and start again.

**Step 3: Carve the outline.**

Using the #699 carbide tapered bur, carve only the outside edge of the leaf pattern. Hold the drill perpendicular to the carving surface and plunge the bur about 1/8" deep. Do not force the bur. Just let the drill do the work and guide it around the leaves. Pull the drill towards yourself for better control.

**Step 4: Score the inner lines.**

Using the #699 tapered carbide bur at a 45-degree angle, score the inner lines of the leaves and the acorns with the edge of the bur. Only carve deep enough to leave witness marks once the stencil is removed.

**Step 5: Remove the stencil.**

Remove the stencil using your fingers. If any gummy residue is left behind from the stencil remove it with a small amount of rubbing alcohol and a clean rag.

**Step 6: Stipple carve around the pattern.**

Use the #4 carbide round bur carve around the outside of the leaves and acorn using a stippling* method. Carve deeper in the lobbed areas of the leaves for more depth.

*Stippling is a dotted like pattern achieved by using a up and down motion while carving with a round bur.

**Step 7: Undercut the lowest leaf.**

Using the large course grit diamond football bur at a 45-degree angle carve an undercut that separates the lowest level leaf. Carve this cut about 1/8 inch deep.

**Step 8: Undercut and separate the acorn.**

Continuing to use the coarse grit diamond football bur at a 45-degree angle carve an undercut that separates the acorn. Carve this cut a bit shallower than the last cut in step 7 keeping the top leaf on a higher layer.

**Step 9: Shape the leaves.**

Continuing to use the coarse grit large football diamond burr at a 45-degree angle blend the undercut into the rest of the leaf by working from the undercut groove outwards using light strokes. Keep shaping until the undercut and the shape of the leaves blend together.

**Step 10: Separate the acorn cap.**

Still using the coarse grit diamond football bur at a 45-degree angle, undercut the acorn cap separating it from the acorn body. The acorn is the highest layer of the carving. Therefore the cuts will need to be the shallowest yet.

**Step 11: Shape the acorn.**

Shape the acorn using the coarse grit diamond football bur. Round the edges of the acorn then blend the acorn shape using light small strokes.

**Step 12: Sand the carving.**

Using the large medium grit football diamond bur, in a handheld pin vise, manually sand the leaf and acorn surfaces until fairly smooth. Work the sanding strokes from the outside edges of the leaves in towards the middle with a slight upper angle. This will help give the leaves a more realistic texture.

**Step 13: Draw the leaf and acorn details.**

Using a lead pencil lightly draw the veins of the leaves. Draw the veins so they flow with the shape of the leaf. Draw the crosshatching of the acorn cap.

**Step 14: Carve the leaf and acorn details.**

Using the #7901 carbide pencil point finishing bur trace the pencil lines carving the veins of the leaves and the acorn cap crosshatching. The lines only need to be shallow surface scratches.

**Step 15: Clean the carving.**

Using a stiff bristle brush scrub the carving to remove any fuzzies. Use compressed air to blow away dust as necessary. I'm using a denture brush in the photo.

## Dental Drill Art

**Step 16: Condition the wood for staining.**

Using a pre-stain conditioner, seal the carved area and let dry for about 10-15 minutes or per the manufactures recommendations. This will prevent the wood from absorbing too much of the color allowing for variable shades.

**Step 17: Mix the color.**

Squeeze a small amount of burnt umber artist oil paint onto a piece of disposable cardboard or thick paper. Using a stick or pallet knife mix in the polyurethane until it becomes about the consistency of ketchup. I prefer using Windsor & Newton artist oil paints.

**Step 18: Paint the low areas.**

Using a small artist paintbrush apply the mixture into the low areas of the carving. This is the outside stippled area and the undercut area around the leaves and acorn.

**Step 19: Blend the color.**

Using a clean rag pull a bit of color out from the lower undercut leaf carvings where we added the color in step 18. Blend the color out with light touches from the dry rag. Add color to the acorn cap and blend with the rag. Leave the stippled area dark.

**Step 20: Touch-up and let dry.**

Returning to the small artist paintbrush add color back in as necessary to keep the low areas the darkest. Once finished, let the paint mixture cure for a minimum of 24 hours or until dry to touch.

## Finished Photos:

# Oak Leaves

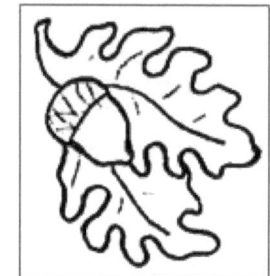
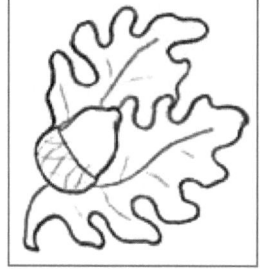
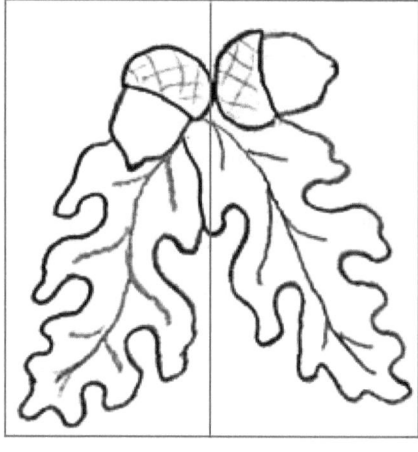
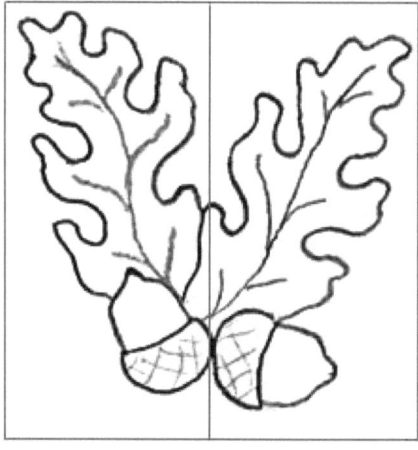
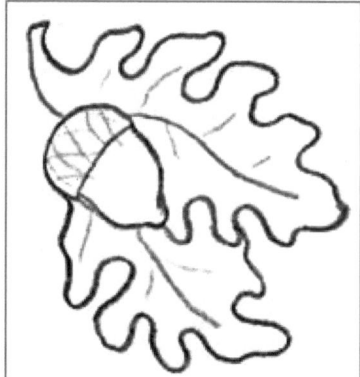
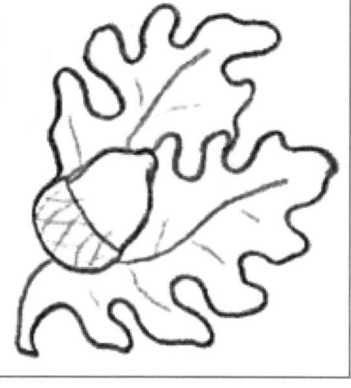
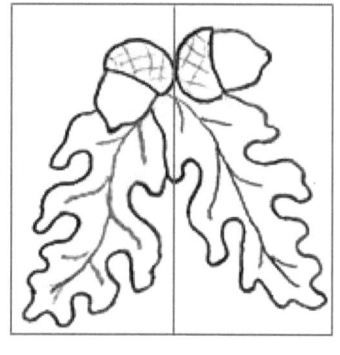
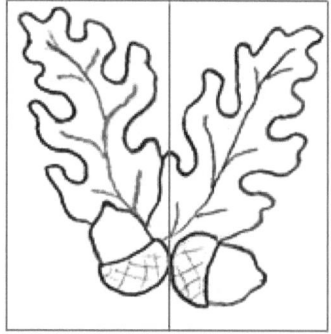

# 3. Eggshell Carving – Random Circles & Bands

Let's carve an eggshell. In this demo I use a goose egg but you could apply this process to any eggshell that is thick enough to carve. This is a fairly simple project but you can use these same methods to layout and carve many shapes and patterns.

This project took a few hours for me to carve. Please remember to check and drain your moisture trap as necessary. Also, stand up and stretch ever so often. Keeping yourself loose and comfortable is important.

**Supply List**

- Goose eggshell (clean and drained)
- Wide rubber band
- Lead pencil
- #699 carbide taper bur
- High speed dental drill system
- Toothbrush (soft)
- Kitchen Cleanser
- Wire or string
- Bleach
- Semi-gloss clear acrylic spray

**Safety**

Please review the section on eggshell carving and personal safety prior to performing this project. Be sure your eggshell has been sterilized prior to carving. Wear a respirator and use a dust collector.

**Step 1: Wrap the rubber band around the eggshell.**

Place the rubber band flat around the center of eggshell length. Once centered straighten the rubber band. Take your time and get it straight and centered dividing the egg into equal halves.

**Step 2: Trace each side of the rubber band.**

Gently trace down the edges of the rubber band all the way around the eggshell. Make sure to trace both sides of the rubber band. Be sure not to move the rubber band as you trace.

**Step 3: Move rubber band and trace into quarters.**

Reposition the rubber band creating another band that divides the eggshell into equal quarters. Repeat step 2 and trace each side of the rubber band.

**Step 4: Move rubber band and trace into eighths.**

Reposition the rubber bands again dividing each quarter into equal eighths. Then trace the rubber band. Repeat for the next set of quarters.

**Step 5: Remove rubber band.**

Once all of the bands are traced your eggshell should look like the picture. There should be 4 bands going all the way around the eggshell creating eight equally spaced football shaped areas.

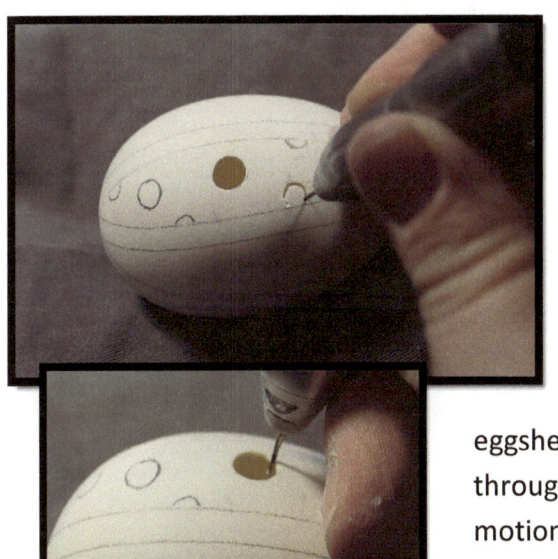

**Step 6: Draw circles inside the eighths and cut.**

Draw 5-7 random circles roughly about a 1/4" in diameter inside one of the areas between the bands using pencil. Make a few of the circles cut off by the bands (D shaped). Keep the pattern random.

Use the #699 bur and the dental drill cut the circles out. Hold the bur perpendicular to the eggshell and gently push it down until it penetrates through the shell. Then cut out the circle in a clockwise motion. If the bur produces any burn to the eggshell switch to a new bur immediately.

**Step 7: Carve smaller random circles filling in around the larger circles.**

Using the #699, cut randomly sized smaller circles filling in areas between the bands. Keep all of the circles from overlapping and leave enough "meat" so they are not too fragile.

**Step 8: Repeat for each eighth section.**

Repeat steps 6 and 7 until all of the areas between the bands are filled with various sizes of circles in random patterns.

Be sure to keep making a few circles that are cut off by the bands (D shape). This helps to define the bands.

**Step 9: Clean off pencil marks.**

Using warm water and a toothbrush gently scrub with a kitchen cleanser to remove the pencil markings. Once all of the markings are removed rinse off the remaining cleanser under the warm water.

**Step 10: Soak in bleach.**

Carefully attach a thin wire or string to the eggshell so it can be used later to lift the egg. Place the eggshell in a container and completely cover the eggshell with bleach. Let the egg soak 8-12 hours. The bleach helps to whiten the shell but also smooth's out the rough edges around the carved areas. If there is any of the inner membrane left in the egg the bleach will dissolve it away. After the eggshell has soaked rinse with warm water and air dry. Be sure to follow all of precautions and warnings of your bleach.

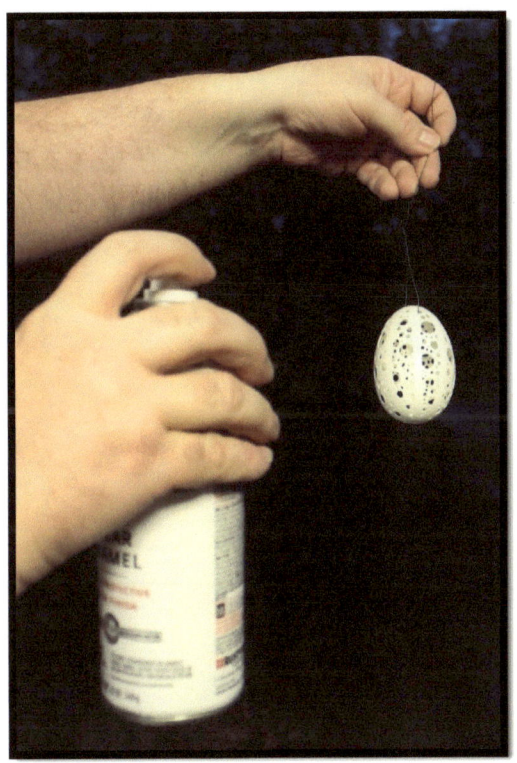

**Step 11: Seal the eggshell.**

Holding the eggshell using the thin wire (or string) spray the eggshell with clear enamel and let dry. The enamel protects the shell and keeps it from discoloring over time. Please follow the directions on your can of spray enamel.

## Finished photos:

## Examples of the circle pattern

# 4. Glass Engraving- Falling Leaves

Let's engrave some leaves in glass. In this example I will engrave a wine glass but this method will work on about any pieces of glass. I found this wine glass in a discount store and thought the green color would go well with some tree leaves. I picked oak leaves because that is what was lying in my backyard.

When engraving on glass you will need to be sure not to apply too much pressure. The burs can build up heat and can crack the glass. Glass varies in quality and thickness. You will need to evaluate your piece.

This project took a few hours for me to carve. Please remember to check and drain your moisture trap as necessary. Also, stand up and stretch ever so often. Keeping yourself loose and comfortable is important.

**Supply List:**

- Colored wine glass
- Printed artwork on full sheet sticker paper or stencil film
- #8 round carbide bur
- Flame shaped green stone bur
- High speed dental drill system
- Scissors
- Dry erase marker
- Glass cleaner
- Paper towels

**Safety:**

Please be sure to wear a dust mask or a respirator. Glass dust has been associated with respiratory disorders. I am not aware of any dental drill artist having issues but let's be sure to keep it that way. Refer back to the personal safety section if needed.

### Step 1: Print the stencil

Print the oak leaf artwork onto a full sheet of sticker paper or stencil film. Reference the "Image Transfer" section for greater details.

### Step 2: Apply artwork to glass

Cut out the leaves making individual stencils. Remove the backing paper from the leaf stencils and apply them to the wine glass. Arrange them on the glass keeping the pattern and size random.

Hint: If you softly stick each stencil on a piece of cloth before putting it on the glass it will leave less gummy residue once removed. I generally soft stick them to my jeans before applying them to the glass.

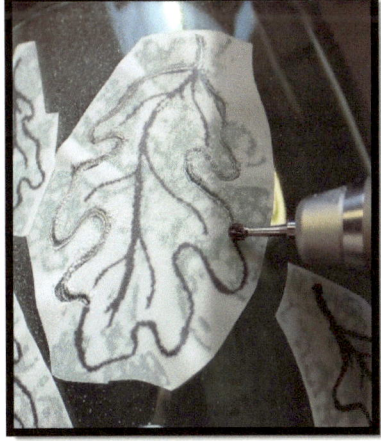

### Step 3: Engrave the outline

Using a #8 carbide round bur engrave the leaf outline through the stencil. The #8 works best when held at a 45-degree angle. Remember, you will have more control over your lines if you pull the drill towards your body.

**Step 4: Remove the stencil**

Using your fingers, remove the stencil. If any gummy residue is remaining on the glass just wipe it away using a paper towel.

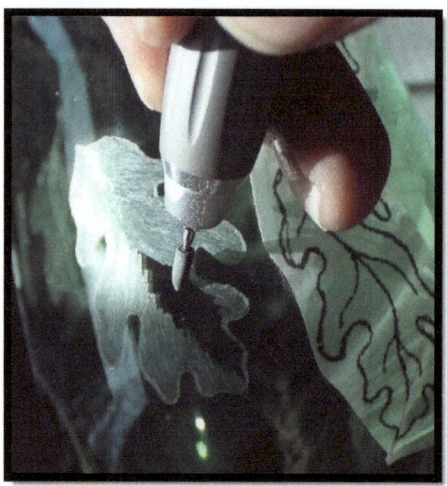

**Step 5: Engrave the inside of the leaf**

Using a flame shaped green stone bur, engrave the inside of the leaf. Holding the bur at a 45-degree angle, use a soft touch to color in the inside. The green stone will leave a frost like texture to the surface of the glass. Be sure you get the entire inside area engraved.

**Step 6: Engrave the veins in the leaf**

Sketch the leaf veins directly onto the engraved leaf using a dry erase marker. Try to draw the veins similar to the artwork. Keep them flowing with the leaf shape.

Switch back to the #8 carbide round bur and engrave the veins.

**Step 7: Repeat steps 1-6 for each leaf**

Repeat the engraving process from steps 1-6 until all of the leaves are complete.

Clean the finished piece with glass cleaner and a paper towel.

# Finished photos:

## Glass Engraving- Falling Leaves Pattern

# Conclusion

Engraving and carving with the dental drills can be a very rewarding hobby but most importantly have a good time and be creative. There are always a few bumps along the way but, for me, the enjoyment far outweighs the negative.

As I'm sure you have realized, the dental drills can be used on a variety of materials and objects. The opportunities really are endless for the dental drill artist. Carve or engrave the subjects and items you find most interesting and appealing. Personally, I enjoy carving nature and wildlife on natural objects like gourds, antler, and eggshells. I have found that if you have a personal connection with the subject or the object you are carving or engraving you will be more engaged and do better work.

The old saying is "practice makes perfect." I hate this saying. Perfect is an unachievable goal. There is no such thing as perfect. Even the best artist will find something wrong in their works. If someone ever achieved perfect there would be no challenge left to overcome. I prefer the saying "practice makes progress." This is an achievable goal. Continue to practice your carving and engraving and you will continue to progress in your skills. Compare your work to where you were last month, or last year, or from wherever you started. If there is progress then your doing it right.

# Resources

Below is a list of resources I have researched at some point in my dental drill art journey. I do not endorse one over the other. This is just a list of companies for your high-speed engraving and carving consideration.

**High Speed Engraving Systems and Supplies:**

These companies sell the handpieces and the accessories to get you going as a dental drill artist. Most specialize in the high-speed engraving and carving field and provide almost all of the supplies you will need.

- Graphic Transfer, **http://www.graphictransfer.net**
- Profitable Hobbies, **http://www.profitablehobbiesstore.com**
- SCM High Speed Engraving, **http://www.scmsysteminc.com**
- Sculpting Studio, **https://sculptingstudio.com**
- Treeline USA, **https://www.treelineusa.com**
- Turbo Carver, **http://www.turbocarver.com**
- Utah Handpiece Repairs, **http://utahhandpiecerepair.com**

**Dental Drill Burs:**

Below are a few dental supply companies from where I have purchased burs. Generally, the dental supply companies have the best deals on burs. Remember to search for FG (friction grip) burs rated for 300,000- 400,000 RPM's when buying for your artist dental drill. Both of these companies have a good product catalog. I would suggest you get a copy for your shop.

- Dental Burs USA, **https://www.bursusa.com**
- Midwest Dental Supply, **http://www.mwdental.com**

## Handpiece Parts and Repairs:

Repairs to the handpiece turbine is a specialized area and Russ at "Utah Handpiece Repairs" is the only one I can find that does this type of work for the artist style dental drills.

- Utah Handpiece Repairs, **http://utahhandpiecerepair.com**


## Gourd Carving Supplies:

As I stated earlier, gourd carving is an industry of its own. There are many places to buy gourds and gourding accessories. Here are just a few I have used in the past.

- Arizona Gourds, **http://www.arizonagourds.com**
- The Caning Shop, **http://www.caning.com**
- Welburn Gourd Farm, **http://www.welburngourdfarm.com**
- Wuertz Gourd Farm, **http://shop.wuertzfarm.com**


## Training DVD's:

There is a limited amount of training DVD's that are dedicated to dental drill art. Of what is available here are a few I own and found helpful.

- Gunstock Basket Weave and Fish Scale by Joe Cummings, **http://joecummingsstudio.com**
- A Trip Through The Script, Upper and Lower Case Lettering by Ken Brown, **http://utahhandpiecerepair.com**
- The Call by Craig Hone and Robin Coalson, **http://profitablehobbiesstore.com**

**Royalty-Free Artwork**

Below are a few resources you can use to find royalty-free artwork.

- iStock, **http://www.istockphoto.com**
- Dreamstime, **https://www.dreamstime.com**
- Shutter Stock, **https://www.shutterstock.com**
- Art Design Studio, **http://artdesignsstudio.com**

**Want more Dental Drill Art?**

If you want to hang out with other dental drill artist please ask to join the "Dental Drill Art" Facebook group. We are a group of dental drill artist who help each other out, share new projects, and just talk shop. If you have read this far in this book, I would say you would fit right in!

**Want to keep in touch with me?**

If you would like to find out what I have been doing since I finished this book, here is where you can find me on the web.

- My website: **http://rogerwolfordstudio.com**
- Facebook page: **https://www.facebook.com/CarvingsbyRogerFWolford**
- YouTube page: **https://www.youtube.com/user/rfwolford/videos**

www.ingramcontent.com/pod-product-compliance
Lightning Source LLC
Chambersburg PA
CBHW040054160426
43192CB00002B/62